HIDE & SEEK SCIENCE™

Where's That Bat?

by Barbara Brenner and Bernice Chardiet

Illustrated by Carol Schwartz

Cartwheel BOOKS®

SCHOLASTIC INC.

NEW YORK   TORONTO   LONDON   AUCKLAND   SYDNEY
MEXICO CITY   NEW DELHI   HONG KONG

To Matthew G.
—B.B.

To the bats that save the world
—B.C.

To Len and Randi
—C.S.

Text copyright © 1999 by Barbara Brenner and Bernice Chardiet.
Illustrations copyright © 1999 by Carol Schwartz.
All rights reserved. Published by Scholastic Inc.
SCHOLASTIC, CARTWHEEL BOOKS and the CARTWHEEL BOOKS logo
are trademarks and/or registered trademarks of Scholastic Inc.
HIDE & SEEK SCIENCE is a trademark of Chardiet Unlimited, Inc.

Library of Congress Cataloging-in-Publication Data

ISBN 0-590-12819-1

12 11 10 9 8 7 6 5 4 3 2 1   9/9 0/0 01 02 03 04
Printed in the U.S.A.   14
First printing, October 1999

Introduction

They have soft fur
and wings like leather.
They have bones
light as a feather.

They live in barns
and caves and towers.
They eat bugs or fruit
or flowers.

They hunt by night.
They sleep by day—
upside-down snoozing
is their way!

Some look like vampires!
Some look like mice.
Don't be scared.
They're really nice!

Some are large and
some are small.

Go batty and you can
find them all!

Night Hunters!

It's evening.
A dark cloud streams out of
a church tower.
It looks like a flock of birds.
Now one flutters past a street light.
It's after that moth!
Do you see that?
It's a Big Brown Bat!

It's a Fact:
Although they fly, bats aren't birds.
They're mammals, who nurse their young.
This bat is the one you're most likely
to see in your neighborhood.
In spite of its name, a Big Brown Bat is quite
small.
Its body is only about as long as a crayon.
And it's quite harmless — except to bugs.
A Big Brown Bat can eat more than
five hundred insects in an hour!

Name That Bat!

These aren't Halloween masks!
Believe it or not, they're real bat faces.
Their names are a clue to which is which.
There's a Leaf-nosed Bat, a Dog-faced Bat,
a Spear-nosed Bat, and a Wrinkle-faced Bat.
Can you match each name to a face?

It's a Fact:
There are more than 900 different kinds of bats.
Some bats have big ears or a "nose leaf"
to help them hear.
Other bats have big eyes to see with.
Not one of them is "blind as a bat."
And in spite of their scary looks,
bats are actually shy, gentle animals.

Foxy Bat!

Flying Foxes are the largest bats in the world.
Like many other bats, they sleep during the day,
hanging upside down.
Flying Foxes sleep in trees,
where they look like folded umbrellas.
Do you see five Flying Foxes sleeping?

It's a Fact:
There are about 60 different kinds of Flying Foxes.
Some have wingspreads of up to six feet!
These giants of the bat world eat fruits and blossoms.
If a Flying Fox finds a tree full of juicy fruit,
it sometimes saves some in its cheek pouches
to eat later.

Visit From a Vampire!

This pig is sleeping.
It doesn't know that it has a visitor.
But if you look carefully,
you'll see a Vampire Bat
getting ready to have dinner!

It's a Fact:
Vampire Bats live on blood.
A Vampire Bat will land near an animal,
walk up its leg or back, and
make a cut with its sharp teeth.
Then the bat sticks its tongue into the cut,
and laps up the blood.
In spite of its weird habits,
the Vampire Bat is *not* a monster.
It will share food with other Vampire Bats.
It will come to another bat's aid.
And a female will often adopt
an orphan Vampire Bat baby.

Fisherbat!

A Fishing Bat is "singing for its supper."
As it skims over water, it makes a
high-pitched sound that humans can't hear.
When the sound hits an object like a fish,
it echoes back and the bat can tell exactly
where the fish is.
Do you see the fish that is going to be this
bat's supper?

It's a Fact:
The way bats use sound to find food
is called echolocation (say eh-koh-loh-KAY-shun).
Bats that use echolocation to hunt their prey
are usually bats with big ears.
The better to hear with, my dear!

Bat Babies!

These bat babies — called pups —
hang out in the cave while their moms
are off hunting insects.
Now the female bats are back —
and they're looking for their pups.
How many mother bats are looking?
Do you see one baby that has been found?

It's a Fact:
The mother bat finds her pup by calling.
The pup hears her voice and chirps back.
The mother flies toward the sound
and smells the pup to make sure it's hers.
Then she nurses, cleans, and grooms it.
It's amazing that bat moms and pups find
each other.
There can be as many as 250,000 bats
in a single cave!

Minibat!

This tiny cave-dwelling bat spends
its nights catching *very* tiny insects.
It's sometimes called a Hog-nosed Bat.
If you find it, you'll see why!

It's a Fact:
The Hog-nosed Bat of Thailand
is the smallest bat in the world.
It's only as big as a bumblebee
and it weighs less than a jellybean.
It is very rarely seen.
Scientists think it may soon be extinct.

Snake Attack!

As the sun goes down,
hundreds of fruit bats
swarm out of their cave.
Watch out, bats!
There's danger twined in the vines
at the cave's entrance!
Do the bats see it?
Do you?

It's a Fact:
Every evening snakes gather at the mouth
of a certain cave in Puerto Rico.
As the bats fly out, the snakes strike!
The unlucky bats are squeezed to death
in seconds.
Then the snakes eat them, wings and all.
In a short while, some satisfied snakes
crawl away to digest their meal.

Yum! Yum! Cactus Flowers!

These two bats are feeding on saguaro cactus flowers.
If you look closely, you can see the long tongue of one bat reaching into a flower.
The other bat seems to have yellow powder all over its head.
Do you see it?

It's a Fact:
Many desert flowers open at night.
Then bats come to feed on nectar —
the sweet liquid in the flowers.
As they feed, the bats carry pollen
from one plant to another.
Passing the pollen around makes it possible
for the plants to produce new plants.
In this way bats help more than 500
different kinds of plants to survive.

Tagging the Bat!

Ssssh! The bats on this wall are sleeping!
They're holding on with their feet, so they
don't fall.
Three of the bats have bands on their legs.
Do you see the three banded bats?

It's a Fact:
By banding bats, scientists can follow
their movements and find out where they go.
They know that many bats stay asleep
in the same place during cold weather.
But they've discovered that these snoozing
Pipistrelle bats just take "bat naps."
They keep waking up, moving to a new place,
and then going back to sleep.

Bat-tent! Cool!

It's broiling hot here in the jungle.
But this Leaf-nosed Bat
has made a shady tent
for itself up in a palm tree.
Can you find the bat's penthouse?
Do you see its leaf-nose poking out?

It's a Fact:
A few bats make temporary "homes"
to protect themselves from the weather.
This bat from Mexico and South America
bites a palm leaf with its teeth
until the leaf folds over
to make a flap.
Presto! A private tent!

Who Eats WHOoooo?

Somewhere in this pile of leaves,
you'll see a beetle and the scorpion
that's about to eat it.
But the scorpion could be eaten by the bat!
Or, the hungry owl could get to the bat first.
Can you find all these hungry hunters?

It's a Fact:
Owls do prey on bats.
But people are probably the bat's
worst enemies.
In some places, people kill bats for food.
In other places, they poison them or
destroy their roosts,
because they think that bats are dangerous
or that they carry disease.
The truth is — bats are clean, gentle creatures
that do much more good than harm.
They help trees, and plants, and people.

Technicolor Bats!

Here are bats from many parts of the world,
flying in to show their true colors!
If you look sharp, you'll find a Red Bat,
a Speckled Bat, an Orange Bat,
a Yellow-shouldered Bat, and —
guess which one is called the Ghost Bat!

It's a Fact:
Color is good camouflage for many animals.
Often it protects them from being seen.
The Speckled Bat is pretty hard to see
in dappled sunlight.
And the Yellow-shouldered Bat can hide in
a bunch of bananas —
and have a good meal while it's hiding.

Bat Bedtime!

The sun is just coming up.
Time for all good bats to head for home.
But where is home?
If you look carefully, you'll see
seven different places a bat can call home.
One of them is a house made just for bats!

Bats can live in barns, church towers, attics, hollow trees, bat houses, and living trees.

Fishing Bat

Flying Fox

Brown Bat

Hog-nosed Ba

Long-nosed Bat

Puerto Rican
Fruit Bat

Pallid Bat

Speckled Bat

Yellow-shouldered
Bat

Pipistrelle Bat

Leaf-nosed Ba

Orange Bat

Ghost Bat

Spear-nosed Bat

Red Bat

Mexican
Freetailed Bat

Tent building
Bat

Dog-faced Bat

Vampire Bat

Wrinkle-faced Bat